Table of Contents

The Coldest Continent 4

Finding Antarctica 10

Earth's Laboratory 14

Visiting the Bottom of the World 20

Plants and Animals 22

Glossary 30

Index 31

Show What You Know 31

Further Reading 31

About the Author 32

Unlike Earth's other continents, Antarctica has no countries. An international agreement signed in 1959 called the Antarctic Treaty preserved the continent entirely for scientific research.

The Antarctic Treaty was originally signed by Argentina, Australia, Belgium, Chile, France, Japan, New Zealand, Norway, Russia (then-USSR), South Africa, United Kingdom, and the United States. The treaty now includes more than 50 countries, with membership still growing.

The Coldest Continent

Welcome to the coldest and windiest place on Earth! Antarctica is the planet's fifth-largest continent. And though it's covered in ice, it is the world's largest desert! The Antarctic polar desert covers the 5.5 million square mile (14.25 million square kilometer) continent.

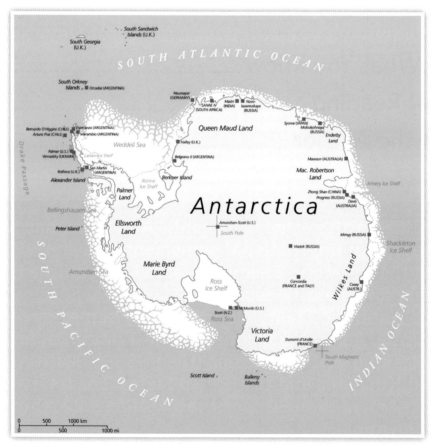

The southern end of Earth's axis, the South Pole, is in Antarctica.

Antarctica's ice sheet is about a mile (1.6 kilometers) thick on average. But it's about three miles (4.8 kilometers) thick in some areas. The continent contains about 90 percent of the ice on Earth.

A desert is defined by its low levels of **precipitation**, not its temperature. A desert gets less than 10 inches (25 centimeters) of precipitation each year. Antarctica gets an average of about 6.5 inches (16.5 centimeters) per year. Most of it falls as snow.

Brrr! Antarctica's average annual temperature ranges from about 14 degrees Fahrenheit (–10 degrees Celsius) on the coast to minus 76 degrees Fahrenheit (–60 degrees Celsius) at the highest parts of its interior.

The lowest temperature recorded on Earth's surface at ground level was minus 128.56 degrees Fahrenheit (-89.2 degrees Celsius) at Russia's research outpost Vostok Station in inland Antarctica on July 21, 1983.

ANTARCTICA

REESE EVERETT

Rourke
Educational Media

rourkeeducationalmedia.com

Before Reading:

Building Academic Vocabulary and Background Knowledge

Before reading a book, it is important to tap into what your child or students already know about the topic. This will help them develop their vocabulary, increase their reading comprehension, and make connections across the curriculum.

1. *Look at the cover of the book. What will this book be about?*
2. *What do you already know about the topic?*
3. *Let's study the Table of Contents. What will you learn about in the book's chapters?*
4. *What would you like to learn about this topic? Do you think you might learn about it from this book? Why or why not?*
5. *Use a reading journal to write about your knowledge of this topic. Record what you already know about the topic and what you hope to learn about the topic.*
6. *Read the book.*
7. *In your reading journal, record what you learned about the topic and your response to the book.*
8. *After reading the book complete the activities below.*

Content Area Vocabulary
Read the list. What do these words mean?

dehydrate

dormant

hydroponic

international

precipitation

rumored

semi-aquatic

speculated

terrain

venture

After Reading:

Comprehension and Extension Activity

After reading the book, work on the following questions with your child or students in order to check their level of reading comprehension and content mastery.
1. What makes Antarctica different from other continents? (Summarize)
2. How could melting ice in Antarctica affect other parts of the world ? (Infer)
3. How much daylight does Antarctica get in the winter? (Asking Questions)
4. How does Antarctica's climate compare to where you live? (Text to Self Connection)
5. Why is it important for people working in Antarctica to eat high-calorie foods? (Asking Questions)

Extension Activity
Imagine you are going to spend the summer at a research base in Antarctica. What will you pack? What will you study? What kind of adventures might you have? Write a story about your imagined experience. Perhaps you'll solve a mystery or make an amazing discovery!

The air in Antarctica is so dry, a person can **dehydrate** just by breathing. And it's windy! Antarctica has the highest recorded wind speeds of all Earth's continents. Wind speeds can be faster than 62 miles (100 kilometers) per hour for many days at a time. Some researchers go to Antarctica just to study wind.

Antarctica's frozen landscape is one of Earth's largest volcanic regions. In 2013, scientists discovered an active volcano under the mainland ice sheet. In 2017, they discovered 91 new volcanoes in West Antarctica, where there now are 138 known volcanoes. It's unknown if these newly discovered volcanoes are active.

Mount Sidley is Antarctica's highest **dormant** volcano. It is a member of the Volcanic Seven Summits, the highest volcanoes on each of the seven continents.

Antarctica has only two seasons: winter and summer. During the summer, Antarctica is on the side of Earth tilted toward the sun. It's daytime for six months. During the winter, Antarctica is on the side tilted away from the sun. It is dark for these six months.

Finding Antarctica

With the harsh winds, extreme cold, and long, dark winters, it's no wonder Antarctica has no permanent residents! Unlike the other continents, Antarctica has no countries. It is governed by an **international** agreement signed in 1959 called the Antarctic Treaty.

Antarctica has never had a native human population. Scientists say the continent broke off from a larger land mass called Gondwana before humans evolved in Africa millions of years ago. There were no land bridges to Antarctica, so early humans couldn't migrate there like they did to other regions.

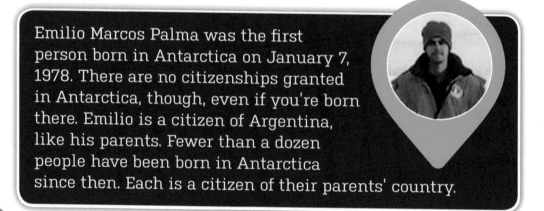

Emilio Marcos Palma was the first person born in Antarctica on January 7, 1978. There are no citizenships granted in Antarctica, though, even if you're born there. Emilio is a citizen of Argentina, like his parents. Fewer than a dozen people have been born in Antarctica since then. Each is a citizen of their parents' country.

Before humans found Antarctica, people speculated about a continent existing at the bottom of the Southern Hemisphere. They called it *Terra Australis Incognita*. This means "unknown southern land" in Latin.

CONTINENTAL DRIFT

Pangaea

Laurasia and Gondwana

Modern World

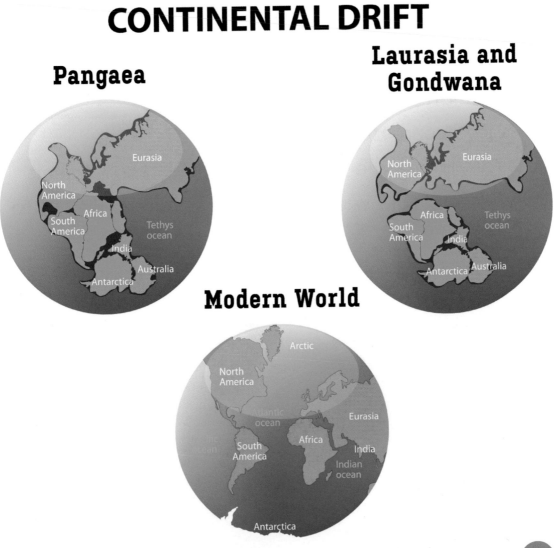

In the 1770s, British explorer James Cook (1728 – 1779) spent three years trying to find the **rumored** continent. He crossed the Antarctic Circle but couldn't navigate the icy ocean. He gave up on finding the land mass, but his tales of seals in the frigid waters drew ships full of hunters to the area.

American explorer and seal hunter John Davis (1784 – unknown) is credited by some as the first to set foot on the continent. He and his crew landed on the shore of Hughes Bay in 1821.

Historians do not all agree John Davis was the first to reach Antarctica. There is still some debate.

Earth's Laboratory

Antarctica is the only continent where no war has waged. The 1959 Antarctic Treaty made it a demilitarized zone. The international agreement preserved Antarctica entirely for scientific research.

A researcher sits still as an emperor penguin checks him out.

A cargo ship carrying research station supplies is prepared for unloading.

Antarctica is one of the world's most important natural laboratories. Unlike other continents, it is mostly untouched by humans. Scientific studies done there often cannot be done anywhere else. Antarctica also drives Earth's climate and ocean circulation. Change on the continent affects the entire planet. Antarctic research helps scientists understand global environmental issues such as climate change, sea level rise, and ozone depletion.

The United States now has three year-round Antarctic research stations. Australia and Britain each has four. In all, dozens of countries maintain permanent research outposts.

About 4,000 people live on these research bases in the summer. About 1,000 staff the stations in the winter. They study everything from geology to climate change to space weather.

A cheerful red research station in Antarctica stands out against the snowy landscape.

Scientists explore an area of terrain not covered in ice.

The people who live on Antarctica's research stations eat a lot of frozen, dried, and canned foods flown in from their own countries. The closest grocery stores are thousands of miles away! Some stations also have **hydroponic** greenhouses where fresh produce is grown.

Greens are grown in a hydroponic greenhouse in Antarctica.

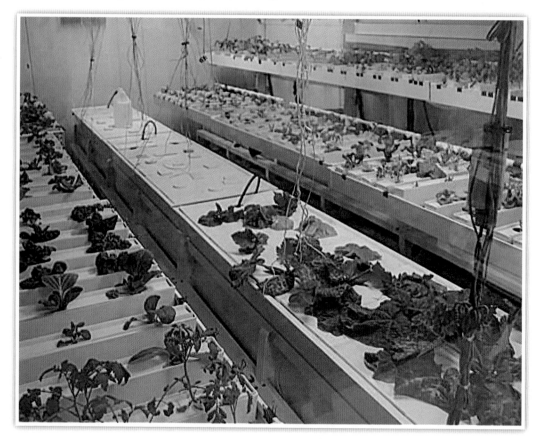

Pemmican is a mix of protein and fat made from dried meat. Originally made by North American Indians, it is considered the ultimate survival food.

Food is the body's first line of defense against the polar climate. Getting the right amount and the right kind is vital for survival. People working in Antarctica's harsh conditions must eat foods with plenty of calories. Chocolate bars, nuts, and energy bars are staples. So are pemmican and sledging biscuits.

Visiting the Bottom of the World

Antarctica is Earth's most difficult landmass to reach. Still, more than 30 thousand tourists visit every year! Most **venture** to the region on cruise ships. Private planes take visitors deep inland. Fewer than 500 tourists a year visit the continent's interior.

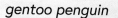
gentoo penguin

The International Association of Antarctica Tour Operators (IAATO) works with the Antarctic Treaty Parties to minimize environmental effects of tourism.

Plants and Animals

Antarctica's wildlife is sparse. Even roaches can't live there, and they can live everywhere! The continent's only true insect is the Antarctic midge. It is less than a quarter inch (0.64 centimeters) long, but it's Antarctica's largest terrestrial animal. That's because its other animals are **semi-aquatic**.

The Antarctic midge eats algae, bacteria, and penguin waste.

With only about two percent of its land not covered in ice, there's not much space for plant growth. There are only two flowering plant species on the continent: Antarctic hair grass and Antarctic pearlwort. These plants are found along the warmer western Antarctic Peninsula and on some of the surrounding islands. Antarctica's other vegetation includes fungi, lichens, and mosses.

Antarctic pearlwort

Antarctica's icy **terrain** doesn't support most wildlife. Antarctic animals live mainly in the surrounding ocean waters, which are warmer than the frozen land.

A humpback whale emerges near a kayaker.

Of the 17 species of penguins in the world, only a handful live in and around Antarctica. Adélie and emperor penguins are the most common.

Adélie penguins live in large groups called colonies. A colony might include thousands of birds.

Chinstrap, gentoo, and macaroni penguins breed on the tip of the Antarctic Peninsula. All species except emperor penguins spend most of their lives at sea.

macaroni penguin

Crabeater seals are thought to be the most social of the Antarctic seal species.

Six species of seals also call Antarctica and its surrounding waters home. They spend most of their time under the sea ice, where it's warmer. Seals give birth on land or ice floes. They also spend time above water soaking up the sun!

Antarctic seals do not have land-dwelling predators. This means there are no animals hunting them when they're out of the water. Researchers say they have little fear of humans for this reason.

Crabeater seals and other species are protected by the Convention for the Conservation of Antarctic Seals.

Activity: Blubber Glove

Penguins, seals, and other animals that live in freezing temperatures have a layer of fat called blubber that keeps them warm. How does it work? Let's find out!

Supplies:
- vegetable shortening
- 2 sealable plastic quart-size bags
- duct tape
- bucket or large bowl of ice water

Directions:
1. Add a large scoop of vegetable shortening to one of the plastic bags.
2. Place second bag inside the shortening in the first bag.
3. Fold the tops of the bags together and seal with duct tape to keep the shortening between the two bags, and the second bag open like a glove.

Experiment:
1. Put your bare hand in the ice water. What does it feel like? How long can you stand to keep your hand there?
2. Dry your hand, then put the blubber glove on. Put your gloved hand in the ice water. What does it feel like? Can you keep it in the ice water longer?

How It Works:
The vegetable shortening is a fat like blubber. It keeps the heat from your hand in, and the cold from the ice water out. This is how animals such as penguins and seals can live in freezing temperatures.

Recipe: Sledging Biscuits

Eat like an Antarctic explorer! Whip up a batch of sledging biscuits and take them along for hikes, bike rides, and campouts.

Ingredients:

1 ¼ cups (150 grams) whole wheat flour

½ teaspoon (2.3 grams) baking soda

½ teaspoon (2.85 grams) salt

2 tablespoons (28.25 grams) unsalted full-fat butter

3 ¼ tablespoons (48 milliliters) cold water

Directions:

1. With adult permission, preheat oven to 375 degrees Fahrenheit (190 degrees Celsius).
2. Using a sieve, add flour and baking soda to mixing bowl. Add salt.
3. With clean hands, rub butter into the mixture until ingredients resemble breadcrumbs.
4. Slowly mix in water. Keep mixing with your hands until you have a ball of dough.
5. Roll out the dough on a lightly floured surface until it's a little less than an inch (2.54 centimeters) thick.
6. Transfer the dough to a lightly greased baking sheet.
7. Cut the dough into 2-inch (5.08 centimeter) squares.
8. Lightly poke each square with a fork.
9. Bake for 15 minutes or until the dough starts turning golden brown.
10. Remove from oven. Allow to cool.

Glossary

dehydrate (dee-HYE-drayt): lose a large amount of water from the body

dormant (DOR-muhnt): a dormant volcano is not doing anything presently but could erupt again

hydroponic (hye-droh-pawn-ik): the process of growing plants without soil

international (in-tur-NASH-uh-nuhl): involving more than one country

precipitation (pri-sip-i-TAY-shuhn): the falling of water from the sky in the form of rain, sleet, hail, or snow

rumored (ROO-murd): told as an unverified account

semi-aquatic (SEM-i-uh-KWAT-ik): partially living in water

speculated (SPEK-yuh-layt-id): made guesses or formed opinions without knowing all the facts

terrain (tuh-RAYN): area of land

venture (VEN-chur): go somewhere or do something daring or exciting

Index

climate 15, 16, 19

explorer 12, 13, 29

native 10

penguins 25, 28

residents 10

seal(s) 12, 13, 26, 27, 28

South Pole 4

tourists 20

war 14

wildlife 22, 24

wind(s) 7, 10

Show What You Know

1. Why is Antarctica important for scientific research?

2. Who was the first person to reach the South Pole?

3. Why must the South Pole sign be moved every year?

4. Can a person be a citizen of Antarctica?

5. What is the name of the agreement governing Antarctica?

Further Reading

Grill, William, *Shackleton's Journey*, Flying Eye Books, 2014.

National Geographic Kids, *World Atlas*, National Geographic Children's Books, 2018.

Seiple, Samantha, *Byrd & Igloo: A Polar Adventure*, Scholastic Press, 2013.

About the Author

Reese Everett is a children's book author from sunny Florida. When she's not researching and writing, she enjoys planning trips around the world. She would very much like to spend a summer working in Antarctica sometime soon.

Meet The Author!
www.meetREMauthors.com

www.rourkeeducationalmedia.com

PHOTO CREDITS: Cover, p1: ©leonello, ©Goddard_Photography, ©posteriori, ©Tenedos, ©KeithSzafranski, ©vladsilver, p4: ©Peter Hermes Furian, p5: ©Andreea Dragomir, ©Kris Wiktor, p6: ©Wiki, p7: ©lucag_g, p8: ©Dan Leeth / Alamy Stock Photo, p9: ©Volodymyr Goinyk, ©H. Mark Weidman Photography / Alamy Stock Photo, p10: ©The Hindu, p11: ©Designua, p12: ©Georgios Kollidas, ©Moritz Buchty, p13: ©David Coleman / Alamy Stock Photo, p14, 15, 17: ©polarman, p16: ©2j architecture, p18: ©Colin Miskelly, p19: ©Jen Arrr, p20: ©steve estvanik, p21: ©chrisontour84, ©evenfh, p22: ©Nigel Cattlin / Alamy Stock Photo, p23: ©Mps197, p24, 27: ©reisegraf.ch, p25: ©Amelie Koch, ©Anton_Ivanov, p26: ©Mariusz Potocki, p29: ©Paul Ward

Edited by: Keli Sipperley
Cover design by: Rhea Magaro-Wallace
Interior design by: Corey Mills

Library of Congress PCN Data

Antarctica / Reese Everett
(Earth's Continents)
 ISBN 978-1-64156-408-3 (hard cover)
 ISBN 978-1-64156-534-9 (soft cover)
 ISBN 978-1-64156-658-2 (e-Book)
Library of Congress Control Number: 2018930429

Rourke Educational Media
Printed in the United States of America,
North Mankato, Minnesota